More Than Sad

Feelings After Someone Special Dies

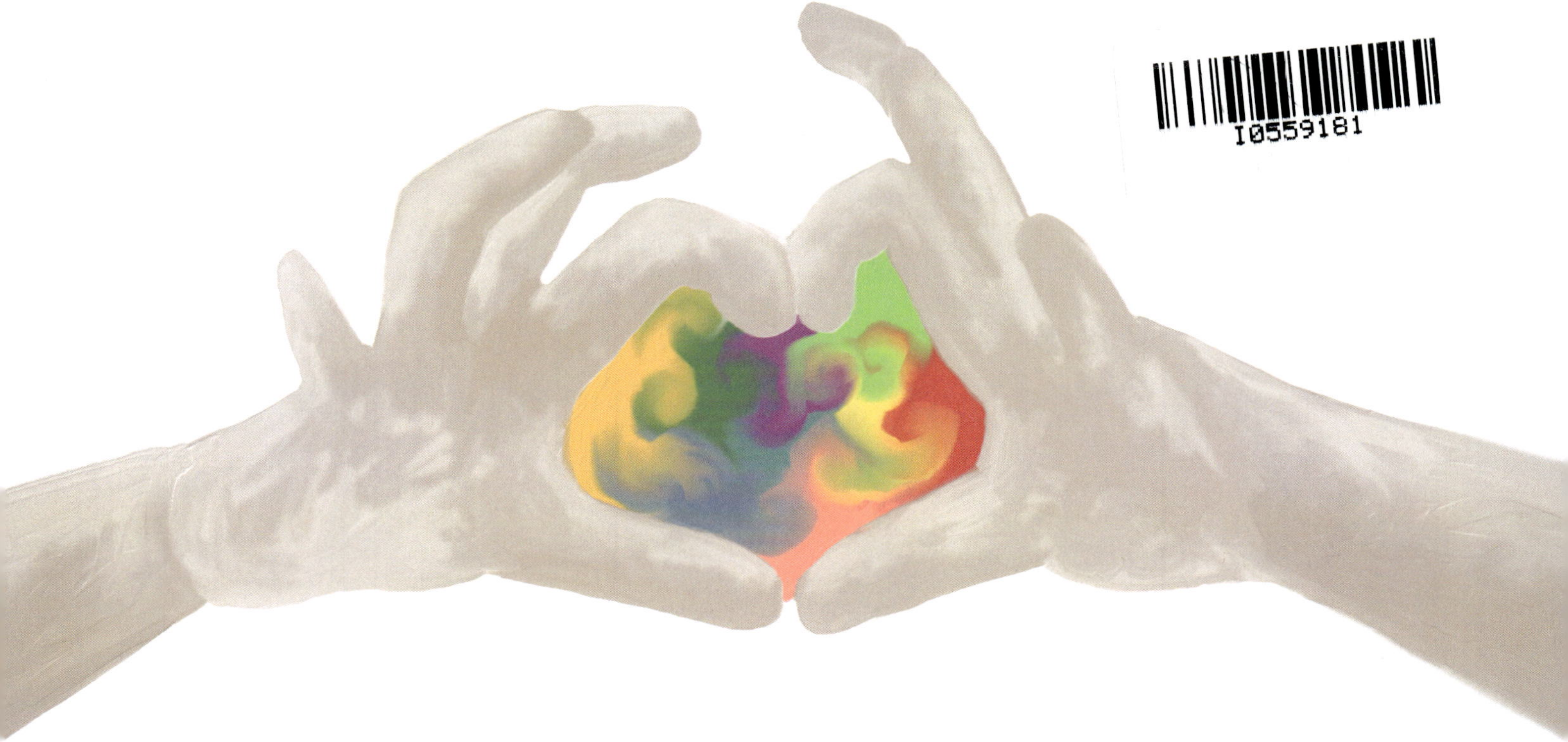

Commissioned By:

www.walkwithyounonprofit.org

Written and Illustrated by
Laura Camerona, CCLS

at

www.wordsworthrepeating.com

Library of Congress Control Number: 2024931928

This book is intended to be read to a child by a trusted adult.

The advice and words within may not be suitable for every child or every situation. In especially stressful or complex situations, this author suggests the involvement of a mental health professional.

Book best suited for children ages 4-12.

ISBN Paperback: 979-8-9873529-4-6

www.wordsworthrepeating.com
Des Moines, IA

Things for Adults to Consider When Reading This Book with a Grieving Child

- Follow the child's lead. If they aren't in the mood to read the book, save it for another moment.

- Oftentimes, bedtime isn't the best time for books about topics that kids may have questions about. It can lead to trouble sleeping. The first time you read this book with your child, try to avoid right before bed.

- Have your child choose a person or people that they can talk to when they have questions or want to talk about their feelings. They may choose their parent, but sometimes, children want to protect their family from being sad and would rather choose a good friend or family member who is less affected.

-Don't expect a certain outward reaction from your child. It is okay if your child doesn't show the emotions that you might expect.

-When each feeling is discussed in the book, consider asking your child or your group one or two additional questions. You can offer kids the opportunity to share their answers, but never push a child to share if they don't want to. Question examples:

Have you ever felt this way?   When do you feel this way?

Where do you feel this in your body?   What are you thinking when you feel this way?

Is there anything that helps when you feel this way?

Activities That Pair Well With This Book

A hands-on activity can be an appropriate way for children to process after reading this book. Children can use colors to symbolize their own feelings. Give kids permission to change what each color stands for. For example, red does not feel mad for everyone. Also, consider asking if they have other feelings not mentioned in the book that they would like to add. After reading this book, consider introducing one of the following activities:

-Color in a human outline showing the different feelings they experience and where they feel them in their body. (A free worksheet is available at www.wordsworthrepeating.com.)

-Create a bracelet that symbolizes how they are feeling. They could use lots of one color and less of another to show what they have been feeling.

-Use a month calendar. Each day have the child color that day's box with the appropriate color(s). Later, revisit to see if they can notice any changes or trends.

-ANY other art project that uses a variety of colors such as a mosaic, abstract art, watercolors, tissue paper candle jars, mixing playdough colors, etc.

In honor of each family who has trusted
Walk With You in their grief journey.
We feel privileged to walk with each family,
past and future, after their devastating losses.
May no family ever have to walk alone.

Someone special died.

I feel sad. We all feel sad.

But, I also feel other things.

When my feelings get big, I can feel
them in different parts of my body.

A big feeling might feel like
a stomachache,
a headache,
an excited energy,
not being able to sleep,
being stuck in a mood,
not being able to concentrate,
or something different.

Each person feels big feelings differently.

I wonder if you have
had these feelings too.

It is normal to have lots of
feelings after someone
special dies.

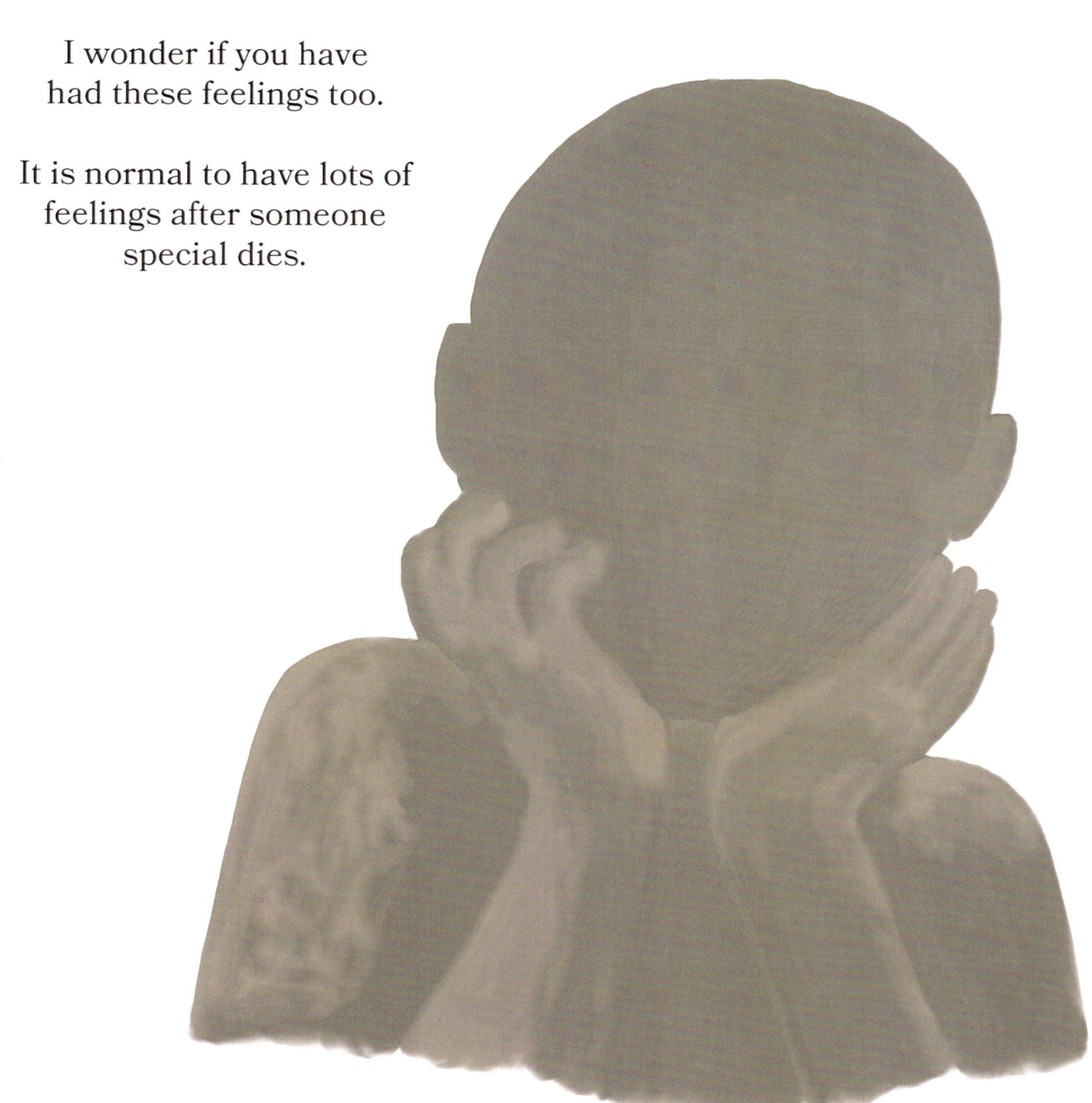

I feel mad. It doesn't seem fair.
I see people everywhere that
didn't have someone special die.
It makes me mad.

Sometimes, you might feel mad too,
and that is okay.

I feel relieved.
It feels good to know that
my person isn't hurting.
They can no longer feel pain.

Feeling something good after someone
special dies can be confusing, but it is
okay and normal to think of good things
about a person's death.

I feel lonely,
and sometimes, I feel left out.
Everyone else still gets to do things
with their person.
It feels like I am the only one who is
missing someone special.

If you feel left out, you are not the only one.
Lots of people feel lonely.

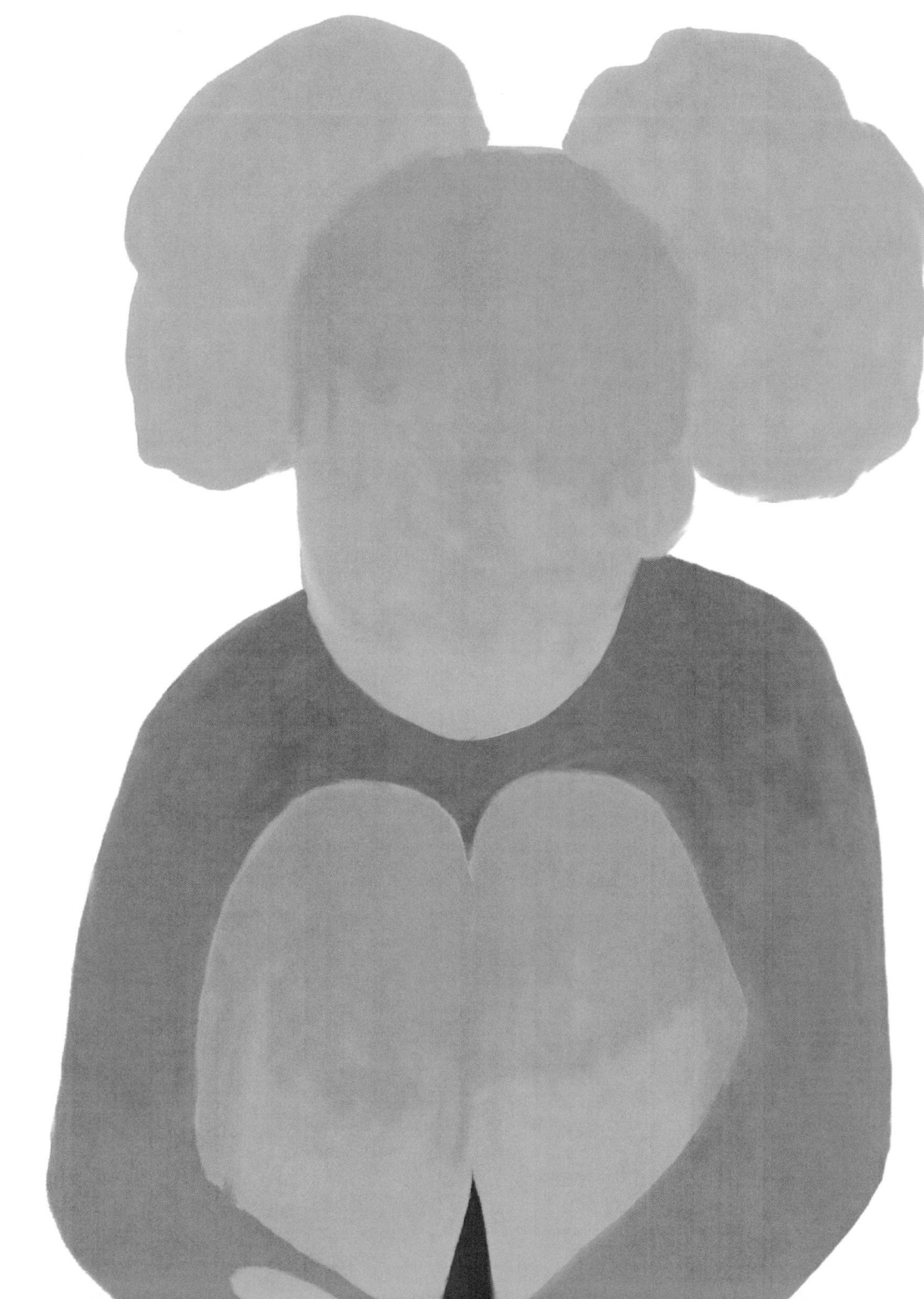

I feel stressed.
I think about my home, my friends,
my family, and the things I like to do.

I worry about my life and how it might change.
Change can be hard.

Different things are stressful for different people.
If you feel stressed,
there are things you can do to help.

I feel curious.
I have lots of questions about death.
Sometimes, I wonder if it is okay to
talk about death.

Adults might not know what to say
because they don't have all of the
answers, but death is something that
you can talk about.
What do you wonder about?

I feel worried.
When someone dies, it can make people worry
about new and different things.

It's normal if you have worries.
Who do you talk to when you feel worried?

Sometimes, I even feel a little bit happy.
I am so happy that my person was in my life.
My memories of them make me smile.
I am happy that they helped me become the
person I am today.

After someone dies, it is okay if you feel happy.
It is still okay to laugh.

I feel hopeful.
I know that there will be some
happier days ahead.
I know that this special person will
always be a part of who I am,
and so, they will always be
a part of my happy days too.

Hope is when you know that good things will come,
even if things feel hard right now.

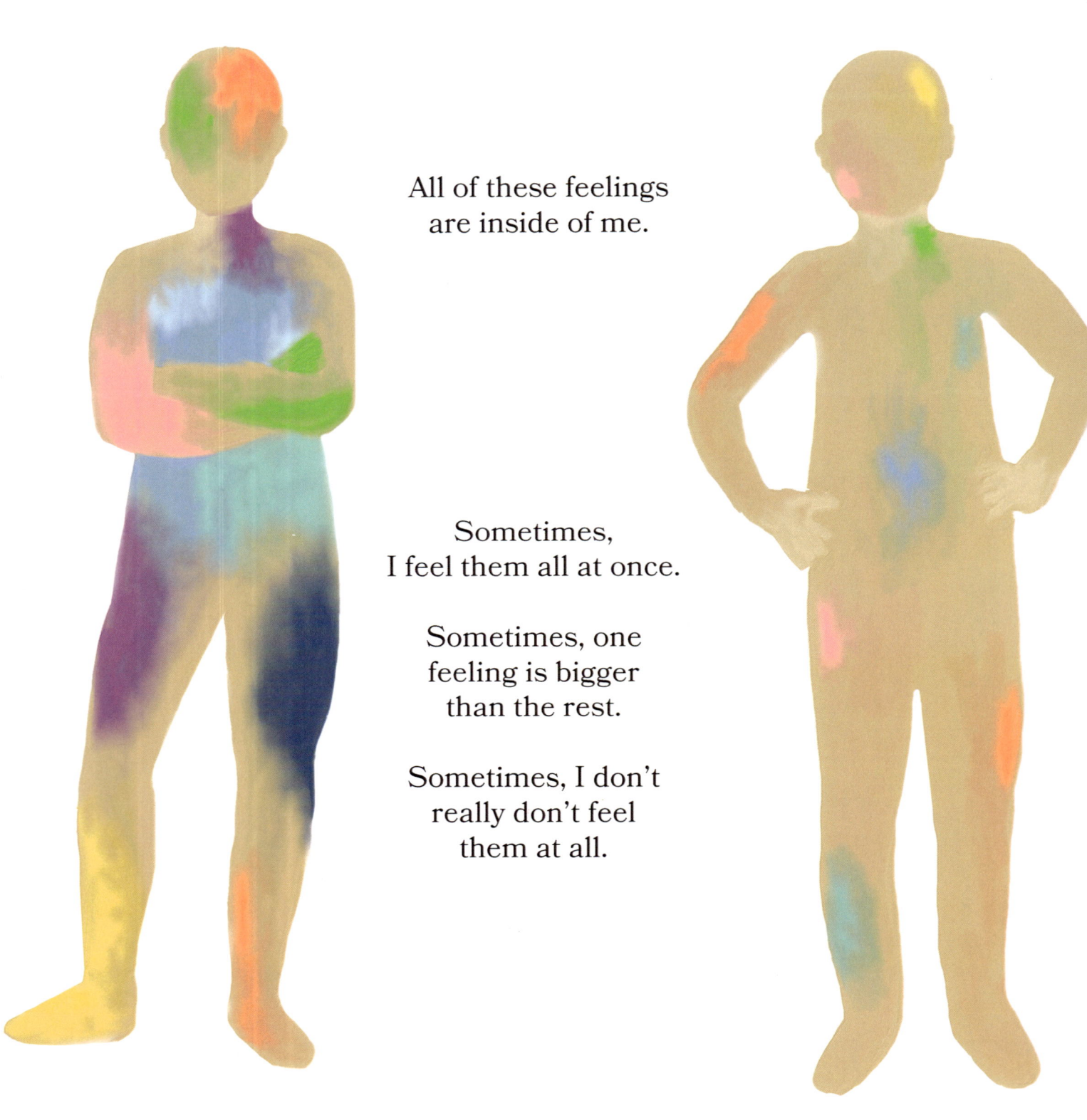

All of these feelings
are inside of me.

Sometimes,
I feel them all at once.

Sometimes, one
feeling is bigger
than the rest.

Sometimes, I don't
really don't feel
them at all.

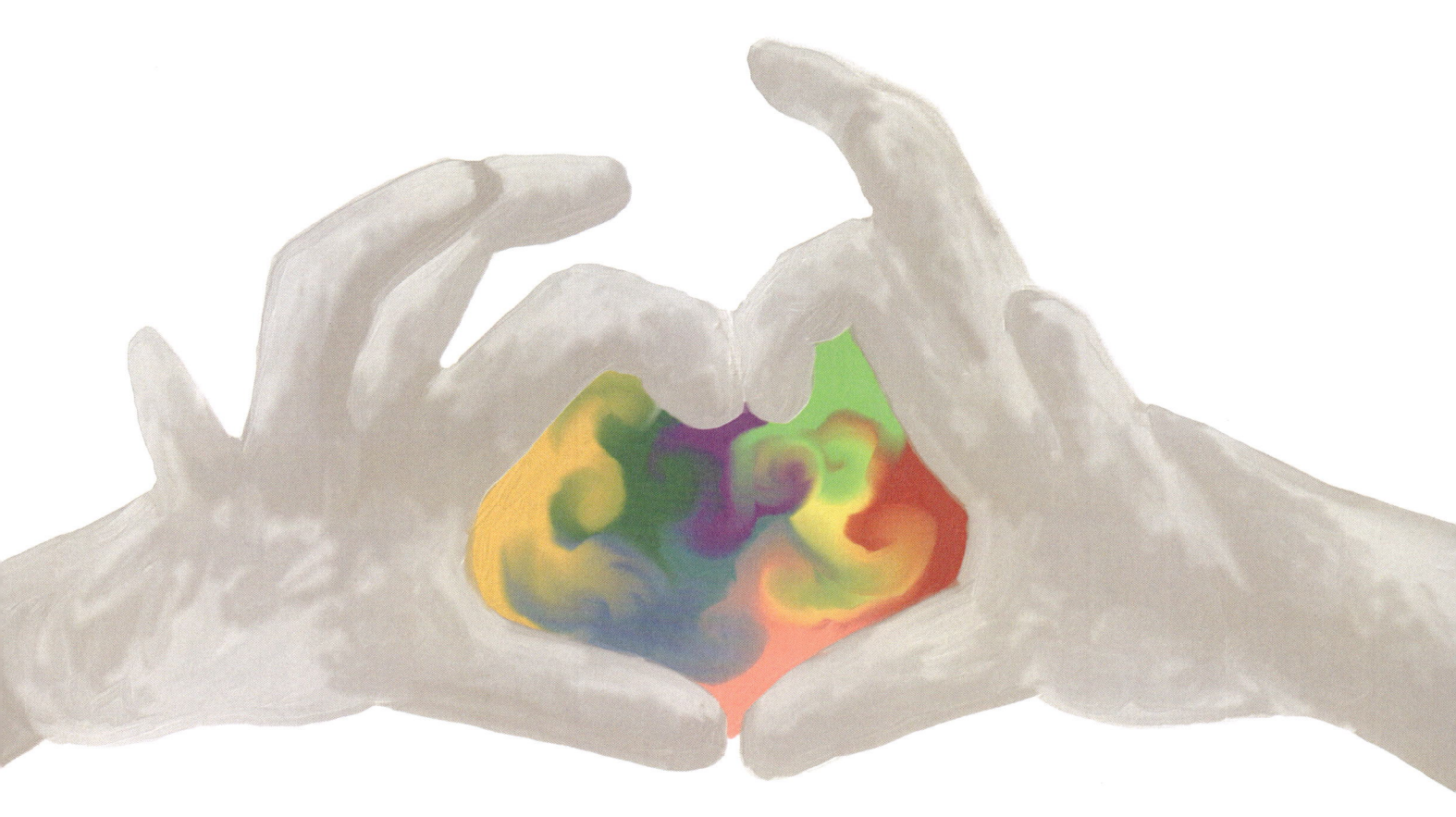

This is okay.

My person will always be special to me
even when the feelings are smaller or
when I don't think about them.

When the feelings get too big,
there are things we can do to help.

Sometimes, telling someone
how I feel can help.
Sometimes, a hug can help.
Sometimes, just being with people
who feel the same way can help.

Each person has to figure out
what helps them.*

After someone dies, all of these feelings
show how special that person truly was.

My special person has become a part of who I am.

My person's special life will be a part of me forever.

* The following pages share some ideas of things that can help with big feelings.

Remember: These ideas might not be enough. A mental health professional can help kids and adults process and work through many feelings. If a child doesn't already see a mental health professional, they can get connected through their school, their pediatrician, or a community grief organization.

Sad:

Find ways to express your sadness. Sometimes, taking time to feel really sad can make it feel easier to carry. Here are some ideas of things that can help when you are feeling really sad:

Journal. Keep it to yourself or share.

Create. Draw, paint, make something with clay. Don't try to make it perfect, just do what feels good to you.

Cry. Some people feel a little better after a good cry. You can set a timer and give yourself a limit, or you can find a time to cry until you can't anymore.

Hugs. Be close to people who care. Ask for a hug or cuddle with someone you love.

Talk. Choose someone you feel good talking with. When you are ready to stop talking about it, you can tell them that too.

Friends. When the time is right, distraction can help. Take a break. Do something fun. It will never mean that you aren't sad anymore or that your person doesn't matter.

Make a memorial. Create an area of your home that you can go when you are thinking of your loved one. You can decorate a jar and put a candle in it. You can decorate a picture frame and put your loved one's picture in it. You can create a garden stone for your yard or plant a tree that you can sit under. Having a special area to remember your loved one can feel like there is a place for the sadness in your life.

Go outside. When sadness is overwhelming, fresh air and sunshine can feel good.

Time does not make sadness go away, but your sadness might feel different with time. There will be times in your life that your sadness feels bigger or smaller. When you are feeling big sadness, know that there will be days ahead when that sadness feels different.

Mad:

When you are mad, it can help to talk about it, but more often, it can help to show it with your body. It can be helpful to get anger out before it explodes. Exploding means that a person can not control their angry actions. Here are some safe things that could help when you feel angry:

Make a target. On the target, write all of the things that make you angry. Fling wet cotton balls at the target or shoot it with water or paint.

Find or make a punching pillow. Find an old pillow or buy one at the store. Decorate a pillowcase with sharpies or tie dye. Hit it as hard as you can, as many times as you want.

Screaming time. Go to your room and shut the door. Scream, yell, get it out! Yelling by yourself in your room may keep you from yelling at friends or family who care about you.

Relieved

Don't feel bad if you are finding some good things about your person dying. Life is full of balance. Although it can be hard to see, nothing is all the way good or all the way bad. It is normal to feel different kinds of relief, including:

Feeling good about your person not hurting. Remember that once a body is dead it does not feel any pain.

Being glad that the death didn't affect other plans. Maybe you are relieved that the person didn't die on your birthday or that you still get to go to your dance recital. It is normal to think about how a death will affect your life.

Stressed:

A death can cause a lot of things to change. It can take time for families to figure out how things will work after the death of a loved one. One of the best ways to help with this kind of stress is to talk about it. Here are some ideas of how to help this kind of stress:

Family conversations. If changes are coming, it is important to talk about them as a family. Make sure you tell your family how you are feeling about these changes. It is also important to talk about how your family will return to your "new normal". Talk to your adult about when and how you want to return to your activities. There is no right amount of time to take a break. Adults can help you work with your school to do what is best for you. If you are worried about grades, you and your caregiver can talk to the school. After a death, many schools can adjust expectations and deadlines.

Have a plan for hard days. What should you do if you decide to go to practice and then you get there and feel like you can't do it? Make a plan for what you should do if you are having a hard time and ask your adult what you should do if you want to leave early.

Practice hard conversations. Think about what you want to tell your friends, classmates, etc. Knowing what you want to say can make you feel less stressed about whether it is going to come up in a conversation. (Even if you have a plan of what you want to say, it is always okay for you to decide that you don't want to talk about it.)

Tip for Families: Say yes to help! When people offer to help or support your family after a death, there are many ways they can help. These are the people that can help get kids to activities, help decorate the house for the holidays, do yard work, help make sure kids have what they need for a new season, etc. If organizing all of this is overwhelming, you could even ask one of these people to help organize the help.

You are not alone, allowing people to walk with you in your grief can ease some of the stress.

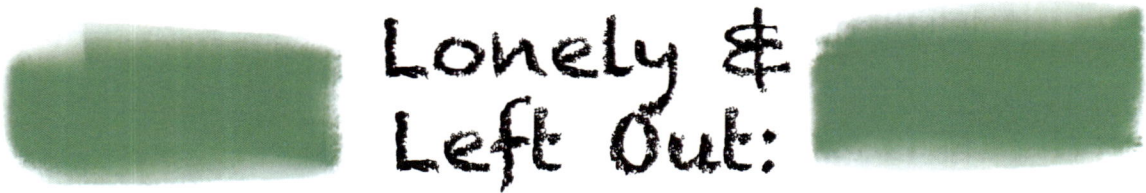

Lonely & Left Out:

When possible, think ahead. As a family, you can talk about different situations that might come up and what you can do to feel less left out. Here are some other things that might help:

Don't keep the death a secret. Many kids think that keeping it a secret will keep them from feeling like the 'weird kid'. You don't have to tell everyone, but it can help to have your adult talk with your teachers and coaches. By telling a few of your closest friends, you can feel less alone.

Think ahead. Talk about different situations that might make you feel left out. Practice different things that you could say when your loved one comes up.

Make a plan for the holidays. Holidays can be especially stressful. When a holiday is coming up, make a plan with your adult. You probably have things that you have always done with your person. Talk about whether you want to keep that tradition or change it this year.

Curious:

When you are curious, it always helps to learn more.

Read a book. There are a lot of books written for kids about death. Your caregiver can help you find good books for your questions.

Visit and ask questions. Many funeral homes offer tours. It can also be interesting to visit a cemetary.

Learn about traditions and cultures. Each culture has different traditions and beliefs about death. Sometimes, learning about these beliefs can help us understand certain traditions.

Remember, there isn't an answer to every question. You might have questions that no one has the answer to. No one knows exactly what it feels like to die. Many people wonder lots of things about death.

Worried:

When you are worried about something, it can be hard to get those worries out of your brain, especially at bedtime.

Talk to someone. Tell an adult you trust about your worries. They might be able to explain something that helps you worry less.

Find a way to get the worries out. Hold a worry stone or a worry doll and focus on giving it all of your worries before you sleep. You could also write them down and then rip the paper up.

Words. Find a prayer, a poem, or a phrase that helps you feel safe and calm.

Tip for Parents:
After a death, kids might worry about how they are going to die. It can help to remind kids that most people die when they are very old. It can also help to have kids think about all of the people in this world that are keeping them safe like parents, teachers, doctors, and community members.

Happy and Hopeful:

Often, happy feelings after a death come from thinking about good memories. Hope can come from knowing your special person would want you to be happy.

Tell people about your person. Your person will continue to make the world a better place when you tell other people about them.

Write and create. When you are thinking about the good things, write them down or create something special. If you feel like it, share what you make with others.

Look through old pictures. This can be a way to focus on happy feelings and memories.

Laugh. If you think of something silly or funny, tell other people. Laugh together.

Keep doing things you love. Remember that your person would want you to be happy.

Wear something that makes you feel connected to your person. You might wear their favorite color or a piece of jewelry that reminds you of them.

Gather with other people who miss your person. Doing this every once in a while or on a special day can help you make new memories and feel connected to your special person.

Walk With You is a non-profit that was founded in central Iowa in 2022. Walk With You commissioned the creation of this book as a way to 'walk with' families with grieving children.

Walk With You believes that no one should have to walk alone. Regardless of a family's background, culture, or set of beliefs, Walk With You meets a family where they are. Whether a family is anticipating the loss of a child, is experiencing the new loss of a child, or is years out from the loss of a child, Walk With You will work to connect them to the support they need.

Learn more about the services and kinds of support they provide on their website: www.walkwithyounonprofit.org

Socials - FB: @Walk With You   Instagram: @walkwithyounonprofit

Words Worth Repeating is an organization that empowers families to have hard and important conversations by creating books that give families the gentle, yet honest words.

Words Worth Repeating partners with non-profits who are passionate and excited about giving families thoughtful resources. In addition, Words Worth Repeating creates custom books for families who can not find the resource they are searching for.

Learn more about the process and browse Words Worth Repeating's many titles on their website: www.wordsworthrepeating.com

Socials - FB: @WordsWorthRepeatingBooks   Instagram: @words.worth.repeating

www.ingramcontent.com/pod-product-compliance
Lightning Source LLC
Chambersburg PA
CBRC090829120626
46547CB00008B/635